HEROES OF AMERICAN HISTORY

Paul Revere
Patriot

Carin T. Ford

 Enslow Publishers, Inc.

40 Industrial Road   PO Box 38
Box 398   Aldershot
Berkeley Heights, NJ 07922   Hants GU12 6BP
USA   UK
http://www.enslow.com

Library of Congress Cataloging-in-Publication Data

Ford, Carin T.
    Paul Revere, patriot / Carin T. Ford.
      p. cm. — (Heroes of American history)
    Summary: A biography of Paul Revere, who is best remembered for his dangerous ride to warn other American patriots that British troops were on the move at the start of the Revolutionary War.
    Includes bibliographical references (p.) and index.
    ISBN 0-7660-2001-0 (hardcover)
    1. Revere, Paul, 1735–1818—Juvenile literature. 2. Statesmen—Massachusetts—Biography—Juvenile literature. 3. Massachusetts—Biography—Juvenile literature. 4. Massachusetts—History—Revolution, 1775–1783—Juvenile literature. [1. Revere, Paul, 1735–1818. 2. United States—History—Revolution, 1775–1783. 3. Massachusetts—History—Revolution, 1775–1783. 4. Silversmiths.] I. Title. II. Series.
    F69.R43 F69   2003
    973.3'311'092—dc21

                                           2002009108

Printed in the United States of America

10 9 8 7 6 5 4 3 2 1

To Our Readers: We have done our best to make sure all Internet Addresses in this book were active and appropriate when we went to press. However, the author and the publisher have no control over and assume no liability for the material available on those Internet sites or on other Web sites they may link to. Any comments or suggestions can be sent by e-mail to comments@enslow.com or to the address on the back cover.

Illustration Credits: *Special thanks* for the lantern image on p. 22 courtesy of the Concord Museum, Cambridge Turnpike, Concord, MA, <http://www.concordmuseum.org>; Courtesy Paul Revere Memorial Association, p. 27; Courtesy Paul Revere Memorial Association, photo © Jim Smalley, p. 15; Enslow Publishers, Inc., pp. 7, 13, 23; The Greater Boston Convention & Visitors Bureau, Inc., p. 28; Library of Congress, pp. 1, 3, 6, 8, 9, 11, 12, 16, 17, 18, 21, 25, 26; *Paul Revere*, oil on canvas, by John Singleton Copley, 1768, Courtesy Museum of Fine Arts, Boston, p. 4; *Old Landmarks and Historic Personages of Boston*, Samuel Adams Drake, Little Brown & Co., 1906, p. 20.

Cover Credits: Inset: *Paul Revere*, oil on canvas, by John Singleton Copley, 1768, Courtesy Museum of Fine Arts, Boston. Background: Library of Congress.

Table of Contents

Paul Revere

Chapter 1

Growing Up

Paul Revere was born on December 21, 1734, in Boston, Massachusetts. Twenty years earlier, his father, Apollos Rivoire, had sailed into Boston's harbor.

The port of Boston was a busy place in the early 1700s. It was often filled with ships from all over the world. Fishing boats delivered their catch of fish, lobsters, and oysters. Cargo boats from faraway countries brought goods such as metal and horses.

Paul Revere's father arrived in the Boston Harbor in 1715.

People, too, sailed across the Atlantic Ocean. They left their homes in hopes of finding a better life in America. One of these was a thirteen-year-old French boy named Apollos Rivoire.

Apollos became an apprentice to a silversmith. An apprentice in colonial times was a worker-in-training who did not get paid. Apollos was fed and housed while he learned how to work with silver and gold.

After several years, Apollos opened his own silversmith shop. He showed great skill in making plates, cups, buttons, pins, and other items.

In 1729, he married Deborah Hitchborn. They went on to have twelve children. Apollos had changed his name to Paul Revere because it was easier for people to say. One of their sons was given the same name as his father.

Little did they know that one day, their son Paul Revere would make the name famous.

Silversmiths make many useful and beautiful items.

In those days, some children started their schooling at a dame school. This was a private school taught by a woman in her home. The students learned reading, writing, and arithmetic.

By age seven, Paul was ready to attend the North Writing School. There he learned grammar, spelling, and geography. Although the teachers were very strict, Paul grew to love books.

Living in Boston was exciting for a young boy. The city's crowded, winding streets were bustling with craftsmen. There were shoemakers, blacksmiths, tailors, bricklayers, printers, and goldsmiths.

This alphabet book is from colonial times, when Paul was learning to read.

Like many boys in colonial times, Paul was finished with school by age thirteen. He began spending his days in his father's shop, learning how to be a silversmith.

Like Paul, many men learned the same trade as their fathers. Here are a brass worker, a shoemaker, and a bricklayer.

Chapter 2

Learning a Trade

Paul worked for the next few years as an apprentice to his father. There was a lot to learn.

He watched his father heat the silver in a large fireplace, called a forge. Sometimes gold was used, but not very often. It was too expensive. Still, some silversmiths called themselves "goldsmiths" because they thought it made them sound more important.

The heated silver became soft. Then it could be formed into a belt buckle, a pitcher, a spoon, or a knife. Paul's father had many tools to cut, twist, and mold the silver into different shapes. The finished pieces were often decorated with designs such as flowers and leaves.

Paul learned how to make silver cups and teapots for fancy tea parties like this one.

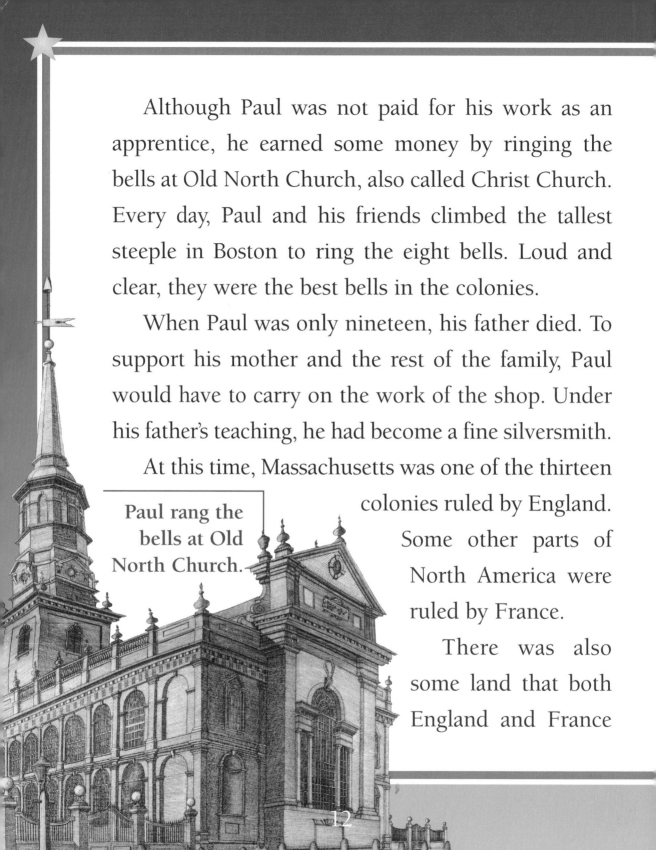

Although Paul was not paid for his work as an apprentice, he earned some money by ringing the bells at Old North Church, also called Christ Church. Every day, Paul and his friends climbed the tallest steeple in Boston to ring the eight bells. Loud and clear, they were the best bells in the colonies.

When Paul was only nineteen, his father died. To support his mother and the rest of the family, Paul would have to carry on the work of the shop. Under his father's teaching, he had become a fine silversmith.

At this time, Massachusetts was one of the thirteen colonies ruled by England. Some other parts of North America were ruled by France.

There was also some land that both England and France

Paul rang the bells at Old North Church.

wanted. They fought over it for many years. This was called the French and Indian War.

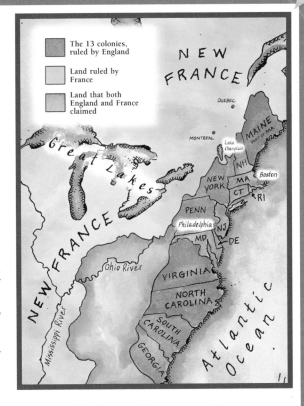

In 1756, twenty-one-year-old Paul decided to help fight. He and about 3,000 other English soldiers started the long march from Boston to Lake Champlain.

They planned to capture a French fort. But on the way, many men began to die from disease. They were also attacked by American Indians fighting on the side of the French. The English soldiers decided to retreat and go back to Boston.

Paul Revere returned to his silversmith business. The care of his mother, brothers, and sisters rested on his shoulders.

Chapter 3

The Coming of War

As a young man, Paul had dark hair, a sturdy build, and muscular arms. He was willing to work hard to be successful.

In August 1757, he met and married Sarah Orne. In the next eight years, Paul and Sarah had eight children. Sadly, two of them died when they were very young. Paul loved all his children very much and called them his "little lambs."

Paul spent every day working in his shop. He repaired items that were broken, like teapots. He also made new serving trays, rings, whistles, mugs, and other silver pieces.

Paul was an excellent silversmith, and he was very busy. His brother Thomas began working for him as an apprentice.

Paul earned money in other ways, too. He taught himself how to make engravings. To do this, he cut words and pictures into thin sheets of copper. Printers used his

This beautiful silver cream pitcher was made by Paul Revere.

engravings to illustrate books and newspapers.

Paul was also a dentist. He carved false teeth from the tusks and teeth of animals, such as hippopotamuses and sheep. Wires were used to attach the teeth inside a person's mouth.

When Paul was not busy in his shop, he attended meetings with important men in Boston. The men included Samuel Adams and John Hancock. They all belonged to a secret group called the Sons of Liberty.

Samuel Adams, left, and John Hancock grew angry with England.

Made up mainly of tradesmen and shopkeepers, the Sons of Liberty met to protest England's unfair treatment of the colonies.

The English had finally gotten the French out of America. But the war with France had lasted a long time. It cost England a lot of money. The English government wanted the colonists to help pay for the war. It placed taxes on goods like sugar, paper, and tea.

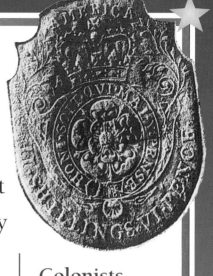

This made Paul and many of the other colonists very angry. They did not want to pay taxes to England when they had no say in the government.

Riots broke out in Boston. In 1770, some colonists threw ice, snow, and stones at a group of English soldiers. The soldiers fired several shots from their guns, and five colonists were killed. This became known as the Boston Massacre.

Colonists were ordered to pay taxes on all paper goods. They were marked with this tax stamp.

Paul made an engraving to illustrate the Boston Massacre. It became his most famous engraving. Many families bought copies to hang in their homes.

To calm down the colonists, the English government got rid of most of the taxes it had placed on goods. But it kept the tax on tea.

The colonists did not think this was fair. They had to come up with a plan to protest the tax on tea—and Paul Revere was right in the thick of it.

"Unhappy Boston!" reads the label on Paul's engraving of the Boston Massacre.

Chapter 4

Messenger for the Revolution

I n 1773, when Paul was thirty-eight, Sarah died. Five months later, he married Rachel Walker. They had eight more children; three died as babies.

Not long after Paul's marriage to Rachel, three ships loaded with tea from England sailed into Boston Harbor. Tea was a very popular drink among the colonists. But they had stopped drinking English tea to protest the tax on it.

Paul Revere's house.

With three ships of tea in the harbor, the colonists decided it was time to take action. On December 16, 1773, Paul and more than one hundred other men dressed up as American Indians. They used burnt cork, grease, or soot to darken their faces. They sneaked aboard the English ships at night and dumped all the tea into the harbor. The event became known as the Boston Tea Party.

Paul left the next day on horseback, riding more than three hundred miles to bring news of the Boston Tea Party to the people of Philadelphia.

This was just one of many rides Paul made delivering news, messages, and important documents among the colonies.

The colonists knew that fighting would soon break out with the English soldiers. America was on the brink of war, and the colonists wanted to be ready. So they stored weapons and gunpowder in the village of Concord across the Charles River.

At the Boston Tea Party, about 10,000 pounds of tea were dumped overboard.

The English soldiers learned of this and wanted to destroy the weapons.

Paul and a few other men knew that the soldiers might attack at any moment. They came up with a signal to warn the colonists across the river. If English soldiers were coming by land, one lantern would be placed in the tall steeple of Old North Church. If they were coming by sea, two lanterns would shine from the steeple.

One if by land and two if by sea: Paul hung lanterns in the church steeple to send a warning about the British soldiers.

The night of April 18, 1775, Paul found out the soldiers would be crossing the Charles River and marching on to Concord. He gave the signal to hang two lanterns. Then Paul put on his riding

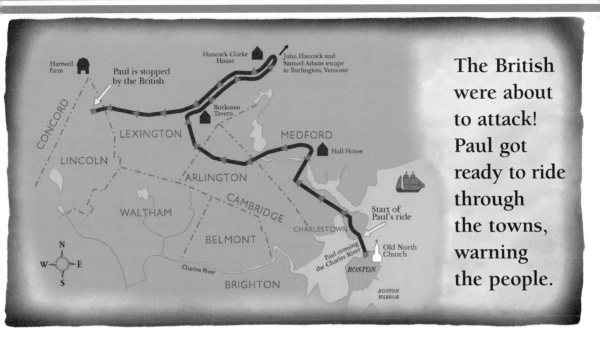

Hartwell farm

Paul is stopped by the British

Hancock-Clarke House

John Hancock and Samuel Adams escape to Burlington, Vermont

Buckman Tavern

CONCORD

LEXINGTON

MEDFORD

Hall House

LINCOLN

ARLINGTON

CAMBRIDGE

WALTHAM

Start of Paul's ride

CHARLESTOWN

BELMONT

Paul crossing the Charles River

Old North Church

N W E S

Charles River

BOSTON

BRIGHTON

BOSTON HARBOR

The British were about to attack! Paul got ready to ride through the towns, warning the people.

boots and went to the north part of town, where he had a boat ready.

When Paul reached his boat, two friends rowed him across the river. There, a horse was waiting for him. Paul would first ride to Lexington to warn John Hancock and Samuel Adams of the danger. Then he would continue on to Concord, spreading the news along the way.

Paul was ready for a night that would go down in history.

Chapter 5

Paul's Midnight Ride

Paul hopped onto his horse and began his ride. Suddenly, two English soldiers began to chase him. Going into a full gallop, Paul escaped.

He rode quickly to Lexington, arriving at midnight. There, he warned Hancock and Adams that the English troops were on the march.

Next, he raced to Concord with two other riders. As they rode, Paul shouted, "The regulars are out!"

The famous ride of Paul Revere.

The Battle of Lexington was the first battle of the Revolutionary War.

Regulars was another name for English soldiers.

In the middle of his journey, Paul was captured. One English soldier told him, "If you go an inch further, you are a dead man!"

The other two riders, William Dawes and Samuel Prescott, escaped. The next day, the soldiers set Paul free, though they took away his horse. As he walked along the road, Paul heard the sound of gunfire. The war for American independence had begun.

During the eight years of the Revolutionary

War, Paul delivered many important messages on horseback. He made gunpowder and helped engrave copper plates, which were used to print more paper money.

Paul also served as an officer in the army. He headed an attack to drive some English soldiers out of Maine. The Americans waited too long to attack, and the English won the battle. It was a disaster for the Americans. They lost hundreds of men, along with ships, cannons, and other supplies. Paul was told to leave the army.

He went back to work at his silversmith shop. He also opened a hardware store and ran a foundry—a metal shop. Many children in Boston enjoyed watching Paul work. Paul always warned them to be

At their foundry, Paul and his son made everything from nails to cannons and church bells.

careful. "If that hammer should hit your head, you'd ring louder than these bells do," he would say. Together, Paul and one of his sons made almost four hundred bells.

When Paul was sixty-five, he opened a mill that made sheets of copper. These were used to make roofs. They were also used to protect the bottoms of wooden ships.

On May 10, 1818, Paul died at the age of eighty-three. He had more than fifty grandchildren.

This statue in Boston honors Paul Revere and his bravery.

Paul Revere devoted much of his life to helping America win its freedom from England. He is best remembered for his midnight ride at the start of the Revolutionary War.

PAUL REVERE

Timeline

1734~Born in Boston, Massachusetts, on December 21.

1747~Becomes an apprentice silversmith.

1756~Fights in the French and Indian War.

1765~Joins the Sons of Liberty.

1770~Makes a famous engraving of the Boston Massacre.

1773~Takes part in the Boston Tea Party.

1775~Makes his midnight ride to warn colonists that the English soldiers were coming.

1779~Leads a failed attack on the English.

1792~Begins making church bells.

1818~Dies May 10 in Boston.

Words to Know

apprentice—A person who is learning the skills for a job. Apprentices did not get paid. They had to train and practice their craft for many years before they were allowed to open their own businesses.

foundry—A shop where metal objects like church bells are made.

French and Indian War—A war from 1754 to 1763 in which France and England fought for control of the Ohio River Valley in North America. Many American Indians fought on the side of the French. Others fought on the English side.

Revolutionary War—A war from 1775 to 1783 in which American colonists fought to be free from England.

silversmith—A person who makes silver items such as teapots, silverware, and whistles.

Learn More

Adler, David A. *A Picture Book of Paul Revere*. New York: Holiday House, 1995.

Fritz, Jean. *And Then What Happened, Paul Revere?* New York: Paperstar, 1996.

Masoff, Joy. *American Revolution: 1700–1800*. New York: Scholastic, 2000.

Wilmore, Kathy. *A Day in the Life of a Colonial Silversmith*. New York: Rosen, 2000.

Internet Addresses

The Paul Revere House
  <http://www.paulreverehouse.org/>

"Paul Revere's Ride" by Henry Wadsworth Longfellow
  <http://eserver.org/poetry/paul-revere.html>

Timeline of the Revolution
  <http://www.pbs.org/ktca/liberty/chronicle/timeline.html>

Index